BUSINESS POISON

DIAGNOSING AND TREATING THE INFECTIOUS POISONS THAT DETERMINE YOUR BUSINESS SUCCESS

JONATHAN MACDONALD

BUSINESS POISON

ISBN: 1493614088
ISBN-13: 978-1493614080

jonathanmacdonald.com

BUSINESS POISON

CONTENTS

INTRODUCTION

The secrets of modern business success can be found within the bloodstream of an organisation. When innovation circulates deep within, market-changing products and services get launched, often to great admiration. When social responsibility courses through corporate veins, lives can change as hope is granted. All of this is wonderfully opportunistic and worth aspiring to, provided that the bloodstream isn't infected by business poison, rendering the organisation unable to function properly.

Business poison is incorrect reasoning in argumentation, resulting in a dangerous misconception. Unfortunately the risk is so high that even the most successful companies are sometimes riddled with business poison that infects multiple parts of the organisation, yet often masquerades as standard business practice. Business poison is subtle, secretive and smart. Throughout decades in business, I've witnessed the wisest executives ingest and digest the worst possible poisons, without even realising the inherent damage they cause to their business. Sadly, I too have been fooled in the past by a range of mistaken beliefs that have had an extraordinarily negative impact on my own businesses.

In this book the poisons and infections will be isolated from the bloodstream and paraded in broad daylight for all to see. From experience it is unlikely that any company is totally immune to this range, yet hopefully you may recognise the signs early enough to combat the damage. In this effort, a number of potential antidotes are on offer that can be used to neutralise the poisons and limit the risk of infections spreading. As business poison is so far-reaching and infection spreads so quickly, now is definitely the right time to read this book in order to keep those business ailments at bay. I hope that every type of decision maker finds significant value here and to those who use this guidance proactively, I am grateful for being able to assist.

To your good health,
Jonathan MacDonald

1. THE POISON OF TECHNOLOGY THAT CAN

When I was younger, the 'cool' stuff was created by large, faceless organisations with brilliant logos and jingles. I imagined they sat in massive offices, smoking cigars, drinking whiskey and dreaming up incredible solutions to problems we hadn't realised we had. Growing up, I found this wasn't too far from the truth – although the non-smoking policy in many buildings diluted the reality.

Let me place down my cards straight away: I love new technology, I'm a geek, and I will pretty much buy anything with some form of wireless transmitter, or trial pretty much any software that increases my productivity.

But equally, I will only keep using stuff that makes my life easier or better… and this is why I have drawers full of useless crap that probably seemed like a good idea at the time. But that's what eBay is for, right?

When speaking with numerous inventors or creators (of whom most were technologists), I realised a while ago, there is a distinct divide in motivation that leads to invention. Without meaning to be too binary, and purely for illustrative purposes, the divide I see is:

1.   Those who create or invent due to an existing problem that needs to be solved
2.   Those who create or invent due to a technological capability, without addressing an existing problem

The justification of the second type tends to be that the technological capability will address a future problem that, maybe, people haven't even realised yet. Actually, most people retrospectively state they are in the first camp – the key word here being retrospectively.

If we look closely at the genesis of ideas, there are multitudes of instances where "doing something really clever with technology" is actually the driver, rather than "doing something that will help or add fundamental value to the end user".

I see it time and time again – the 'adding value' part is appended to the end of a ream of technological wizardry and often, people accept the rhetoric if the powerpoint presentation is cool enough.

In reality I see these as solutions looking for a problem, and, whilst we're on the catchphrases; when you're a hammer, everything looks like nail.

Worse still, if we work for a company or organisation with a strong technological bias, we may well be pre-programmed to dream up a 'use case' or 'user journey' after the technology has already been created (or, at least conceived).

However we arrive at it, these circumstances are symptoms of an exceedingly popular poison known as The Poison Of Technology That Can.

The problem is that the technology around us presents so many opportunities to do 'stuff'; it's very tempting just to go ahead and do it.

We can be driven by the desire for money, the desire for fame, or the desire to fulfil a mandate from our bosses. We can invent stories of demand, which actually are based on an assumption that we represent the mass market.

Rooms of people in corporate suits, earning big money, carrying three smartphones, assuming that the girl on the reception desk truly cares about the latest 3.542v processor that enables something that only those in corporate suits can pronounce, but none are brave enough to describe, in case they get it wrong.

"No, you've misjudged us Jonathan," they say. "The 3.542v isn't for people like her, we are going for the biggest market opportunity, and that is people just like us."

Then I say, "...but, with respect, you may not actually be representative of the biggest market."

Then they say, "No, we are! Everyone I know is like me."

Then I say, "So why are you putting out an advertising campaign aimed at people like the girl on reception?"

Then they say, "Because people like that aspire to be just like us!"

Then I shut my big mouth.

The Poison Of Technology That Can is a terrible virus. It's everywhere you look. Want to test it? Ask someone who has created something, how they came up with the idea. Here are some potential answers:

"We noticed our competitors getting into the space of..."

"We read a report that this market was going to..."

"We were instructed by our CEO that we had to use our tech capability to..."

If the answer starts with phrases like these, it is quite likely they have been infected by The Poison Of Technology That Can.

The evil beauty of this poison is that you can hide it really easily with key messages and marketing communications.

In fact, even people within organisations can believe they are making real people's lives better, simply because they have been told they are.

The poison is so damn clever, it sometimes results in successes, thus justifying future creations based on the same approach of technology first, external purpose second. The poison is also intelligent. It is the big brother of post-rationalisation that continues the viral mutation. So – what's the antidote?

It's as easy and as hard as having the vision, ethical merit and bravery to continually question "how can we make people's lives better?" or "how can we add more value to people's experiences?"

Then, having the courage to invest in fulfilling the external purpose rather than a) following competitors, or b) taking the easy road of doing what's possible, rather than what's valuable.

Sounds easy to say, doesn't it?

Sadly, it really isn't…

However – if you ever wanted a competitive edge, if you ever wanted to tear apart the marketplace you're in, or, most importantly, if you ever wanted to attract loyal and loving fans, my advice is to avoid The Poison Of Technology That Can like the plague.

In fact, Technology That Can will almost guarantee you will be left with a Bank Manager That Can't… and People Who Ignore.

What could be worse?

2. THE POISON OF SINGULAR PERSONAS

The common thinking in big data, analytics and market research is that this modern world of mass connectivity presents a significant opportunity in gaining greater and more valuable insights to the modern consumer/customer/user/individual.

Valuations of social networks through to investment funds into hot funky startups increase as the spreadsheets show rising user numbers coupled with acres of big data.

The advertising industry licks its lips in anticipation of a food bowl full of eyeballs to monetise and companies in the technology industry declare uniqueness at the same time as duplicating the business models of competitors. Meanwhile we, the general public, gleefully use the free services without concern that if a service is free then it is us who are the product.

The new volumes of information drive new volumes of companies such as word-of-mouth agencies and online influencer platforms, whilst every major consultancy publishes reports on how exciting the future will be when we grasp the new concepts (provided you invest into their multi-million dollar help of course).

All the time a dark poison looms under the surface of information overflow. A poison so pungent that the mere mention of it is the metaphorical equivalent of walking into any of the above offices and throwing all the computers out into the car park.

This, my friends, is The Poison Of Singular Personas.

Here's the deal:

The basic view of personal data is that we have a few online profiles and behaviours that show our statuses and preferences. The view is that these are mostly coherent to the actual person in question.

The more advanced view is that we have numerous online profiles and behaviours that together will show our statuses and preferences. The extended view is that some of the information may be exaggerated or incorrect but even so, a 'single customer view' can be constructed so we can understand the actual person in question.

All these views are based on an assumption that a persona is singular, in other words, that the person is the same person, even if their activity happens in multiple locations.

The methodology executed follows in a straightforward way: To get a more complete user profile, one must aggregate multiple data sets and form a picture. You can look at this through different contexts (e.g. discovery mode, interaction mode, purchase mode, etc), but the leading thought is that when it all comes together you get an overall idea of who a person is, what they want and how they operate. This would be fine if it weren't for the fact that it isn't anywhere near the way things really are.

I'd go as far as to say that much of the advertising/marketing industry, many technology corporations and pretty much all of the research industry is based on exceedingly questionable logic when it comes to online user data and insight.

You see, The Poison Of Singular Personas has somehow convinced even the most intelligent analytical thinkers to side-line some major realities, so as to focus on the fashionable hype as outlined above.

So what are these realities? Well, assuming the ideal is for information entered somewhere to be totally true, and let's imagine some people actually do that… the other realities are:

1.   Partially factual information entered by a human (or groups

of humans)

2.   Totally fictional information entered by a human (or groups of humans)

3.   Partially factual information entered by a non-human (e.g. a computer programme)

4.   Totally fictional information entered by a non-human (e.g. a computer programme)

This presents a serious problem we could name 'The Reality of Multiple Personas' which kicks up a whole load of dust in the face of almost every single piece of prediction/assessment/leading thought being touted around today – let alone almost every corporate valuation in new media and many investments made in every industry vertical across the globe. A small issue this is not.

In the mathematics of probability, anything less than 100% likelihood (e.g. 99%/98%) is the same as 0% certainty. It is this simplicity that unfortunately disables the assumption of singular personas. For instance, if on Facebook there is a 1% or more chance that 1 of the above 4 realities is in place, there is equally as large a chance that it is 99%, 30% or 1%. Very clever analysts will claim that X% of clicks are by robots, or Y% of profiles are fake – the truth is nobody really knows. Without certain knowledge, one cannot be sure. Thus, the reports to advertisers about which users fall into a target group, is littered with incorrect information.

In fact, the reality is so stark that people who base their careers on the poison will defend it to painful degrees. And why wouldn't they? It's like being a professional footballer and all of a sudden I tell you that there are five balls on the pitch rather than one. You look, you see one ball, you argue about the other four – even if you can see them, you dilute their significance due to the level of importance the singular ball has. The only perceivable antidote for this poison is to form actual relationships. Yes, call it science fiction, but my suggested antidote is actually to get to know people.

Ah… for a minute you loved the idea… now you've realised it's a total pain to do so. Think about it, you have a user base of 1.5 million people, how on earth are you going to seriously get to know people? Focus groups? Not so much. No, the reality requires things like:

1. Forming relationships with people as humans, to understand their character and their characters (not limiting understanding people to understanding only humans)
2. Embracing semi-factual information and semi-human information as an inconvenient truth in the information set
3. Adjusting the hierarchical view of dominance above the public, to a more flattened view of being amongst life itself, to be immersed within the modern reality

With other topics like the privacy debate and 'who owns your identity?' it took almost 10 years to mature into meme status. I wonder if this topic will take as long? Whilst you're waiting, check out www.weavrs.com and create your new persona. It's a blast. Your new persona can join and interact with social networks, create a blog and regularly update it and tweet on twitter. All of this whilst knowing that the entire world of big data, analytics and market research are counting your 'profile' as real. Ha! Go play, whomever you are.

3. THE POISON OF ZERO NEGATIVE

Over the last few years, as personal media has emerged, I have spotted a few commonalities in the reports of certain businesses. Without passing judgment on the companies involved, I feel compelled to address the findings that include phrases such as "we haven't had any bad feedback" or "nobody has told us they didn't like it".

This is The Poison Of Zero Negative. The blinding lights of no badness.

You know when you work for a company and you go up to your boss to give feedback about something that isn't ideal and he or she says, "well no-one else has mentioned it"?

That's The Poison Of Zero Negative.

You know when you delay buying car insurance for a while because you haven't ever had a crash so one week won't hurt?

That's The Poison Of Zero Negative.

You know when you think you are really good at something because nobody has told you any different?

That's The Poison Of Zero Negative.

It's monumentally common, dead easy to fall into, and I have to say, it's commercial suicide for strategic planning and doing business. As humans we are tremendously eager to have good results. It feeds our ego. We're not naturally programmed to accept good and bad in equal measure. It is against our nature to classify any outcomes as, simply, different results.

One of the most fearsome activities you can do whilst in a

management role is to ask your staff what you're doing wrong. But actually, if you have the courage to ask (without hiding a threat of disciplinary action if the answer isn't 'right'), you can improve your leadership by leaps and bounds, whilst empowering your staff (which, by the way, is the ultimate in good leadership). I spent the first chunk of my career in a bubble, only seeking positives. Upon reflection (and counselling), I now realise that was mainly down to low self-esteem. Yes, really… but enough about me, how about you? How many decisions are you making that are influenced by The Poison Of Zero Negative? Are you absolutely sure you can justify something solely because you haven't received bad feedback?

The pragmatic antidote to The Poison Of Zero Negative is as follows:

1. Assume that people may have opinions that you don't know about
2. Be aware that even if people use a service or buy a product, it doesn't always mean they like it
3. Avoid justifying a business practice based on a feeling that it is OK because people haven't complained about it
4. Finally, never settle into complacency when something appears to be acceptable. For sure, celebrate for a while, but never settle.

Everything can always be better.

4. THE POISON OF VOLUME

Many years ago in 2007, a report by IEEE Spectrum and World Robotics claimed the global robot population was 4.49 million. This was made up of 950,000 'industrial' robots and 3.54 million 'service' robots (service meaning robots not used for making things in factories but in homes, shops and train stations etc).

The prediction several years later in 2010 was that there were 1.17 million industrial robots and 7.2 million service robots. This would put the global robot population at 8.37 million, almost a 25% year-on-year growth over the prior four years.

Looking at the volume data, the word 'population' immediately triggers our minds to search for similar 'population' related information we have – and this commonly consists of the global human population number (which, at the time of writing, is approaching 7 billion).

The prediction of 8.37 million robots can only be described as a drop in the ocean in relation to the human population, so our perceived importance of a concept like 'robots taking over' is minimal.

How can we evaluate the information if our primary data of these robots is mostly in unit volume rather than capability?

If, for example, the capability of 100 robots of a certain type presents the same effectiveness, accuracy and cost of 50,000 troops in warfare, the defence industry would view the numbers in a totally different way.

If, as a further example, the capability of 300 robots of a certain type presents the same effectiveness, accuracy and cost of the entire metropolitan police force in one of the largest cities in the world, the law enforcement sector could arguably view the rising robot population as 'relevant' to their future.

If, as a final example, the capability of five robots of a certain type presents the same effectiveness, accuracy and cost of the entire workforce in your company, I now have your attention.

Fear not, I'm not suggesting we are all destined to be replaced by robots (yet), but I would like to examine the difference that context makes to volume data that otherwise could be derided or at worst ignored. This, my friends, is The Poison Of Volume.

David Ogilvy said, "Don't count the people you reach, reach the people that count", but nevertheless we are surrounded by big numbers. People justify business models, win investment, get promotions and retain accounts based on volume reported, sometimes with little else.

The Media planning and buying industry is traditionally based on reach and specificity, but, it would seem, in that order. If we can't gain specificity, reach appears to be enough, apparently.

When hiring senior managers, the figures that most impress are those that relate to profit or revenue. We seldom ask whether managed staff were loyal, empowered, respectful and respected.

When buying a car, the figures that most impress are the price (obviously) and the mileage. However, a lesser-rated afterthought is for the way the miles were carried out. You can buy a car with 14k miles on the clock, with no idea that those miles were driven like crazy! You can go by observing the state of the engine, but until smart meters are commonplace, it's largely down to a) believing the service history and/or b) believing the salesperson whose only key performance indicator is to sell the damn thing.

The Poison Of Volume is hard-coded into the very systems we work with and in such a way that even when we realise we are commoditising our true needs, the numbers blind us into a false security.

I feel there is a need for re-prioritisation of meaning in addition to pure volume. The Poison Of Volume dumbs us down and results in desired metrics to be, in many cases, just one solitary number.

This perpetual chase of one number belies other values and misses things of real importance. The winning companies of the present, let alone the future, are those who have a lattice of value, only one component of which is volume. I believe we must add the other dimensions to our base-level approach to truly unlock the meaning and therefore understanding of what's going on – otherwise the robots will do it.

Altissima quaeque flumina minimo sono labi

(The deepest rivers flow with the least sound)

5. THE POISON OF THE UNIQUE

Many companies think they are unique. Maybe it's because of their service offering or maybe due to a revolutionary open-plan office environment that allows 'flat hierarchy'.

Mostly, comments about the uniqueness of a situation are claimed to be geographical. For example, when speaking of a business model from Asia, many companies in the West write-off the information as not being relevant because "we're not in Asia".

Many companies believe their industry is so much more complicated than any other industry. Every industry vertical I know feels some uniqueness due to the amount of regulation/policy/whatever – but actually all industries have such obstacles, albeit different sorts.

This is The Poison Of The Unique.

I feel that all territories can learn lessons from others – regardless of location, development or distance. The poison at play is a dangerously artificial structure, created often as a protection mechanism that limits the need to learn.

Less learning means doing more of the same and keeping things as normal. I believe the willingness to learn from others, without thinking you are totally unique, is directly proportional to enhanced success. Put another way, the willingness not to learn is essentially a proactive choice for failure.

6. THE POISON OF STRATEGIC MISREPRESENTATION

Until a few years ago, the Advertising Standards Authority's (ASA) online remit in the UK only covered paid-for adverts, including pop-ups and banners, but excluded advertising controlled by businesses themselves. Now, the Code of Advertising Practice's (CAP) rules on misleading advertising, social responsibility and the protection of children, extend to businesses' own marketing communications on their websites, as well as marketing messages on other non-paid-for space under their control, such as social networking sites.

The ASA cannot fine businesses but it can ask them to remove the offending material and will 'name and shame' the businesses who have gone against best practice.

Rob Griggs from the ASA says: "The ASA will mostly crack down on misleading statements – for example, if a business makes a claim on a website and it doesn't have the evidence to back up that claim. So if a car retailer claimed it sold the most energy-efficient car of its class and it didn't have any evidence, we would ask them to remove it."

I am in full support of anything that works towards advertising and marketing being legal, decent, honest and truthful, however, I wonder where the ASA are drawing the line on the decent, honest and truthful bit.

At the time of writing there's an advert in the London Underground by an airline company that states they are "the UK's favourite short-haul airline".

Unless you were standing in the middle of the train track (bad idea), you wouldn't be able to read the small print with the naked eye, which qualifies the definition of "favourite". Basically their definition of "favourite" is based on number of passengers.

According to dictionary.com, the adjective "favourite" is actually the "most liked, preferred above all others". So, is this airline in question really the UK's and the web's favourite airline? I'm not here to judge, but it took a simple search online to find acres of contradicting evidence.

But this isn't a chapter about an orange airline. This is a chapter about why some companies claim things that aren't necessarily the truth, representing things in a different way from how things actually are.

This is what I call The Poison Of Strategic Misrepresentation.

Strategic Misrepresentation is actually an economic term, which (to paraphrase Jones and Euske in 1991) is the planned, systematic distortion or misstatement of fact (lying), in response to incentives in the budget process (because they have to).

Despite the origins being in economics, I believe the aforementioned case is one of very many examples of Strategic Misrepresentation. Unfortunately, the approach is a poison for several, blatant reasons.

Let's remind ourselves: business poison is incorrect reasoning in argumentation, resulting in a misconception. The incorrect reasoning that many businesses apply here is that people will feel more attracted due to the misrepresented claims. As it is argued that the majority of people won't realise the truth, the pursuance of misrepresentation seems to hold merit. However, this logic is threatened by elements like:

1. People becoming more aware of misrepresentation, either by general awareness or experiential evidence (e.g. buying a product or service due to a misrepresentation, only to find it's bad, then realising almost everyone else feels the same, thus concluding the advertising and marketing was, in fact, lying)

2. Organisations like the ASA who increase the clamp-down on misrepresentation, naming and shaming offenders publicly (feeding point 1 to some extent)

This poison is so incredibly common it is hard to find many companies that have not, at some point, misrepresented the reality. Let it be known I am not saying all advertising should be stark and fact based (which is the side-line plot in the brilliant movie, Crazy People, starring the legendary Dudley Moore).

There is a school of thought that believes that ultimate transparency is not a good thing. The poison I outline here though isn't arguing for, or against, that point. I do believe that transparency and openness are good, but I know for sure that strategic misrepresentation is a sub-optimal way of doing business. There is perhaps nothing stronger than the truth speaking for itself. Aberrations of truth may seem like an easy-win in marketing spin, but I firmly believe it's not the 'one-time' customers you want, it's repeat, adoring customers who can't wait to tell everyone else how much your product or service rocks. Due to this, we are all in the business of positive relationships that can only be built on trust. People become trusting from consistency and integrity, so the ASA line of "legal, decent, honest, truthful" presents a sound four-pillar approach to build trust.

The Poison Of Strategic Misrepresentation is that strategic misrepresentation does not build trust. Hence, if that is what we are trying to do as businesses, it is a poison to apply misrepresentation in our logic, and rhetoric. So what can be done? I can't persuade you to see the value of building trusting relationships as the primary objective in your business, but if you were to consider it, the way to halt the poison would be as follows:

1. Start the logical thought from trust and work back, when

considering everything you do, make or say as a company. In other words, envisage and plan for people being trusting and advocating of you and construct the products, services and communications that would be required for that to be the outcome.

2. Incorporate a flag system that anyone you work with (including partners, agencies and other stakeholders), can use to flag up instances of misrepresentation. In communication terms, have a constant review of the link between reality and statement.

3. Spend the rest of your career concentrating on creating things of extreme value to people. Leave your job if you work in a place that doesn't. Join a company (or start your own), that does.

4. Finally, never apologise for having the belief that the public deserves more. Believe me, it isn't the most popular of viewpoints in a world of strategic misrepresenters, but ultimately, you are in the right and the truth will out. You may earn less money than your peers, you may not be able to buy that waterside apartment in cash – but your heart and soul will be at peace in the knowledge that you are at least trying to make things better. From living through both sides, I can personally guarantee you it is more fulfilling to live your life that way.

"False words are not only evil in themselves, but they infect the soul with evil" Socrates

7. THE POISON OF SERENDIPITY AMORTISATION

The word amortisation comes from Middle English 'amortisen' – to kill, or alienate. Further, in Anglo-French, 'amorteser' is an alteration of 'amortir' from Vulgar Latin 'admortire'.

It's generally used in finance, but here I'm using it in the context of the volume of serendipity in our lives. I've noticed a trend over the last few years, when talking of personalised solutions that 'know' what you want before you want it, for the challenge to be based on a perceived risk of losing the chance moments, the random moments, the serendipitous happenings, that so colour our dull existence.

It is almost as if solutions that would actually assist our lives are a replacement of serendipity, or that the two are mutually exclusive.

I suspect that some of the fear of losing serendipity is actually a fear of computers (or spies) taking over our existence, and 'normalising' humanity. However, I see a blatant distinction between solutions that enable us to be more efficient, and solutions that remove all serendipity from our lives.

For activities I always do, such as buy the same kind of rail ticket, or reserve the same seat on a plane, I have absolutely no desire for serendipity. I willingly accept that such commodity purchases are devoid of chance; in fact, I want that to be the case.

Alternatively, in meeting new people, sparking up conversation and discovering new music, I embrace randomness. I seek chance and welcome serendipity.

The technologies that I would like to see more of are essentially replicators of the things I don't need to leave to chance. I physically and mentally do not want to go through the rigmarole of mundane tasks, for which I simply want the same thing to happen as before, as quickly and silently as possible. I don't want choice in these instances. I want efficiency.

In contrast (and look how contradictory this is), I don't want to know for sure which personalities I will meet later today at the workshop I'm running. I love the discovery.

I've never been to New Orleans, but when I do, I don't want to know the exact map of where the cool bars are – I want to discover them for myself, by chance. I won't open Google Maps, nor check out Foursquare (or whatever is the 'in' thing that year). Yet, back to the other side, when I'm meeting a business prospect, I want nothing left to chance in terms of location and service.

The Poison Of Serendipity Amortisation is a dust cloud that infects the brains of people who can only think in a polarised view. Those suffering from the poison take unified pieces of information and span them across all scenarios, thus resulting in binary judgment that can only, ever, be at the expense of other reason.

For others with the ability to accept multiple things as valid, despite apparent contradiction, the poison does not exist. I genuinely believe we would find life more pleasant and productive if we were more accepting of other points of view – and for those who do not suffer from the poison, it is our job to try and understand and accept those who do.

8. THE POISON OF THE SELF-SUFFICIENT

There is simply no volume of 'innovation workshops' that will temper the mind-set of "we can do it all ourselves", but there is still validity in wanting to change people's minds from thinking they know everything (and can do everything), to wanting to work with others to propel everyone forward. Even when opinion can be changed, I've noticed this shift is often unrelated to a subsequent change in action, something manifested obviously amongst those who know they shouldn't smoke, but still do.

In business, as in life, acting as if one is entirely self-sufficient is a very dangerous way to be. This is The Poison Of The Self Sufficient.

As it happens, this poison was going to be called The Poison Of Incomplete Knowledge because a characteristic of those with unfulfilled potential is to assume that the required knowledge (to achieve full potential) has already been reached and that all expertise has already been incorporated. But as I wrote that draft, I realised the over-riding factor is the misjudgement that no assistance is required due to being confident in self sufficiency.

Upon inspection there appears to be a gap between the level of understanding and expertise perceived to be important and the level of understanding and expertise that's actually needed to succeed. Even then, having the understanding and expertise isn't enough; it's the integration of this into business-as-usual process that makes the real difference. In numerous meetings and conferences I have seen executives go from being uncertain of what to do, to considering themselves informed and empowered to jump into areas they didn't even know existed shortly beforehand. Often, the same executives are tasked with making advised decisions on things that bear absolutely no relationship whatsoever to their actual skills or experience.

Nevertheless, their senior managers are aiming down a gun barrel waving a newly formed P&L. So you have a choice: do you get brave and work with others, or act like you have everything under control and you are totally on top of it all?

One school of thought would say the second option is better, at least in the short term. It seems the self-sufficiency so often portrayed by those in dire need of assistance is something of a survival mechanism with a generous dose of ignorance.

My father once said, "when things go bad, don't go with them". I remind myself of this on a daily basis. Avoid those destined for disaster.

The way to reduce the poison is to continue being positive and identify those with the humility and courage to work with others. They are the ones with the best chance of success. The short-term, award-winning, attention-grabbing, credit-stealing sycophants are ultimately never around for long. The kudos may shoot like a star in the night, but shooting stars quickly become invisible.

At the end of the day I believe there are people around who genuinely see the value in others, reward others, credit others and are nice to others. In return, these are people who have valuable experiences, get rewarded, get credited where due and people are generally nicer to them in return. This is the club you want to be in. Leave The Poison of The Self Sufficient to those who believe they are self-sufficient. Allow them to do what they wish and you can get on with doing the really important stuff.

9. THE POISON OF PROTECTIONISM

Over time I have published a number of ideas that, one day, may come to life – with or without my personal involvement. These were my ideas that I have no protection over in terms of trademark or patents.

You may wonder why I so openly published these ideas, especially in an environment where people are so protective over their concepts. As it happens, I worked out that for these ideas to take flight, they would require external help. So I could:

1. Speak to people I know, in addition to some they recommend, then get a confidentiality agreement signed and create a working group
2. Keep the ideas to myself and try to execute them myself as the sole owner
3. Share the ideas openly with others and see whether anyone other than me would like to make them come to life

The risk of option 1 is that the people I find on my own may not ultimately be the best people for the ideas. Plus, I don't see a great deal of value in a confidentiality agreement when it is very hard, if not impossible, to prove that someone did or didn't have an idea first. The approach also assumes that the idea is totally unique, which quite honestly is rarely the case.

The risk of option 2 is that it's improbable only you can make everything happen. Omnipotence is an equally vicious poison. However hard you try there still isn't a way of stretching 24 hours into 25 and even if you multi-task your head off, focus is diluted from the moment you start the second most important thing, let alone the third.

The risk of option 3 is that others 'steal' the idea and run with it. This is why so many people don't share with others and produces the worst cases of The Poison Of Protectionism.

However, I'd like to propose a different logic as an antidote to this poison. This is what I call 'The 4 Attitudinal Principles of Invention':

1. It is very rare that an idea you come up with is totally unique. The chances are that someone, somewhere, is already working on it and they may have a greater resource than you, let alone some trademark or patent applications in process. This doesn't mean your idea is less worthy or has less potential, but it does mean you are in good company and maybe the market is already setting its own scene in preparation for your version of the idea to take life.

2. Not everyone is inspired by the same thing. People who happen to hear you speaking about an idea are exceedingly unlikely to stop whatever they were doing and start a whole new project/company/whatever on the basis of hearing you speak. It's not that your idea isn't incredible – I'm sure it is – but people are into different things. Most inventions are too nuanced to be replicable.

3. It's not actually down to the quality of the idea; it's the execution of it. Sure you need a brilliant concept but when it comes down to it, success isn't based on an idea itself. Profit isn't based on the idea itself. Fame isn't based on the idea itself. The way you execute it determines all those factors – whichever one you prefer as your metric of success. If you look at this in the context of the 1st principle (it is very rare that an idea you come up with is totally unique), you could have numerous people with the same idea but the ultimate winner will still be the one who executes best.

4. Talent creates and genius borrows. As it happens,

originality can be a pain. It's harder to prove a business case. It's harder to convince people to invest. It's harder to show people you aren't crazy and ultimately, it's harder to know how the hell to execute as nobody has done so before. As it turns out, many of the ideas around today that have turned into established businesses are based on older ideas, but done better. Google wasn't the first search engine, iTunes wasn't the first music player and Facebook wasn't the first social network. Oh and by the way, I would place money on none of them being the last of their kind, despite being market leaders at the time of writing.

Despite these 4 Attitudinal Principles of Invention, there is an extreme level of protectionism in most industries, especially from people who haven't been in business for a lengthy period. Often, people who are starting up on their own, take a view that the business world is some blood-sucking, evil, idea-grabbing monster which preys upon the young and innocent. Well, from experience, the business world can be like that, but it also exists in the realities of the four principles I outlined above. The truth is that the business world doesn't normally listen to newcomers, especially those with potentially disruptive ideas. If they did, the reality is they mostly wouldn't care a great deal. My advice to those suffering from The Poison Of Protectionism is this:

1. Find something that exists and better it. I'd wager there isn't anything that cannot be bettered. Plus, this way you can always tell people what you are working on because what you are bettering already exists. One caveat is that it is often counter-productive to follow competition. It is far better to create your own playing field, even if you take the ball (and maybe some of the players) from the old one.

2. If you have something you think is totally original and world changing, decide what your ultimate goal is. If your

goal is for the world to benefit from the idea being a reality, don't fear others 'stealing it'. Share it openly and if someone does 'steal it' let's hope they either make it real, or even see the genius you are and invite you to join in. If your goal is to become super-rich and famous for being such a stunning entrepreneur, then either form a secret team or do it yourself in secret. Personally I believe you could get the same result from sharing openly but that requires a certain level of faith and a specific clarity in what your ultimate goal is.

3. Learn 'The 4 Attitudinal Principles of Invention'. These will sanity check your thoughts along the way and who knows, maybe it will make the difference between something being great and a non-launched pipe-dream that you never got round to?

Good luck.

10. THE POISON OF PROOF

Bravery is one of the critical factors in becoming a market leader. Note the word leader as opposed to follower. It's a critical distinction. However, when some companies are trying to justify a venture into the unknown, the most comforting thing is to know that someone else has already tried it. Actually, that someone isn't just anyone – it's usually a competitor. A competitor can theoretically provide proof that something works or doesn't. The competitor is seen as a contextually relevant expert.

This is The Poison Of Proof: A poison that primarily guarantees that others are setting the bar for you. It is a poison because the net benefit of receiving evidence is critically diluted by the fact you are, by design, second place. This is a poison of continuous non-evolution. It is a certification that someone else needs to make the move first, or there isn't enough reason to do so.

My diagnosis is that many companies who ride on this poison are those with a significant blame culture, within an environment where people are very keen on pointing the finger at others, escaping personal accountability. I'm certainly not condoning a disregard of risk, but I am firmly questioning the logic in assuming that those without your specific objectives should be trusted with your strategic direction. This approach is a danger to both innovation and improvement, residing in the knowledge that many companies, especially legacy-based companies, are no longer in the game of winning, but surviving. Survival, apparently, ensures the pension payout, the assured promotion and the promised bonus.

The people who change the world are those who do not seek proof from competitors prior to doing something different. I fully understand the pressures involved and, believe me, I have lived through the politics surrounding corporate decisions. However, at some point you have to ask yourself:

Do I want my market, or my life, shaped by someone else?

Do I settle for something less?

Do I accept that my opinion is worth less than the opinion of someone who doesn't know me, or my company?

It would seem we're eager to spend money we don't have, to buy things we don't need, to impress people we don't care about. Are we running the risk of operating our companies like this? The Poison Of Proof is rife and, for those who adore being second rather than first, it is apparently justifiable on many levels. My advice is this: If you can sleep at night knowing your fate is in someone else's hands, then go for it. If you actually want to make a difference, wake up.

Change, invest, improve, resign, restructure, partner, grow, whatever. But don't, under any circumstance, stay still and let someone else define your life. Let's face it; second place is for people who don't try hard enough – or just aren't brave enough. Personally and professionally, you can choose to be first. It is literally up to you whether you agree with that.

11. THE POISON OF PRESUMED INFLUENCE

Back in 2011, Stephanie Rosenbloom wrote an article in the New York Times entitled "Got Twitter? What's Your Influence Score?". Here is the opening text:

"Imagine a world in which we are assigned a number that indicates how influential we are. This number would help determine whether you receive a job, a hotel-room upgrade or free samples at the supermarket. If your influence score is low, you don't get the promotion, the suite or the complimentary cookies. This is not science fiction. It's happening to millions of social network users. If you have a Facebook, Twitter or LinkedIn account, you are already being judged — or will be soon."

For those of you in the advertising and marketing industry the above is relatively old news. However, I feel it represents a fundamental poison of modern world business that lives on to this day. This is The Poison Of Presumed Influence.

From an advertising and marketing perspective there are three types of media. Owned media (e.g. company owned websites), bought media (e.g. search engine terms) and earned media (e.g. external conversations about your brand). Within this triumvirate it is commonly thought that the public value assigned is lowest in owned media and highest in earned media, with bought media in between.

This makes logical sense. After all, conversations that people have can affect the attitudes and behaviours of others, especially when people trust the opinion or advice of the person speaking with them. However, this is very different to how companies often talk at people, hence people tending to prefer personal conversations over propaganda.

Even though the logic may follow that finding those with influence socially are those who are most powerful at spreading brand messages, identifying some online influencers is only a minor part of accessing the power of earned media. The majority part is what you do next. I have observed the common mistakes organisations make are:

1. Treating the influencers like any other consumer and speaking at them rather than with them
2. Offering influencers incentives that are seen as bribes which does more damage than good
3. Doing nothing other than monitoring the influencers, hoping they advocate and don't turn negative

To properly enter into the world of earned media, an organisation needs to zoom out of the 'social media', 'digital' and 'online' buzz word landscape and address fundamental strategic and organisational paradigm shifts. This includes elements such as assessing the level of porosity your organisation has, accessing and extrapolating the level of ultimate trust in public, creating and implementing engagement protocols, agreeing and testing sign-off processes, authoring and applying crisis management systems, formulating integration into sales conversion, raising staff awareness and infiltrating behaviour mandates, managing the linkage into performance indicators, and so on. This is a brief selection of modern business hygiene factors. There are many more.

My point is, you can start with monitoring and analysis, provided you understand that monitoring and analysis is less than a single percentage of the actual requirement – and even then, as we will see below, it is as far removed from the holy grail as you could possibly imagine.

Much of what we're currently fascinated by in terms of 'influence' is ultimately a warm-up act. A sideshow of persistent inaccuracy.

Imagine I publish a public status update that suggests that a particular device is worth buying and someone else gives a similar recommendation at a conference, offline, on stage.

Let's say the same recipient of influence who reads my status update is in the audience at that conference. They see my update and hear a recommendation from someone else at the same time. If they proceed to buy the device, who is credited as the influencer?

In another, simpler scenario, imagine I am amongst several influencers but I was the one who pushed the recipient into conversion. However, the conversion happened offline, totally unconnected with online behaviour or activity.

In the first scenario I would be the prime influencer as the offline influence at the conference falls outside the remit of online influence. In the second the influence is invisible and the retail strategy may take the credit.

Ask yourself: what would it take for both scenarios to be accurately attributed to the genesis of behavioural change into conversion?

Azeem Azhar, CEO of PeerIndex recognises this, calling it "the Clay Shirky problem," referring to the writer and theorist who doesn't use Twitter much. "He's obviously massively influential," Mr. Azhar said, "and right now he has a terrible PeerIndex." Azhar is suggesting this is Clay's problem and I wonder whether Clay is concerned?

My point is this: if the thing I discuss online, or Clay discusses offline, is converted offline, the only way of tracking influence is to have data sensors on absolutely all physical touch points, linked to absolutely all virtual touch points. This, in addition to CCTV and audio recording devices on every square mile on earth.

Frankly, if those who would like to exploit influence were able to act without regulation and legislation, the ultimate win would be to have sensors inside everybody. Microchips that linked our thought, word and deed. Tracking our every move to place exact accountability on everything. There's a road map for that.

However, there are two significant threats to the effective maturation of this industry:

1. Regulation and legislation may get in the way by limiting what is allowed to be 'mined' for various reasons – one of which could be human rights, another could be the terms and conditions inherent to certain platforms
2. People may decide to restrict access to their information and thus dilute the completeness of the surveyed data

Either threat would significantly distort the data but the second threat resonates strongest for me as I personally believe the noise about how all this gorgeous data contains the "black gold of the 21st century", is fundamentally missing the point that the owners of the goldmines are the general public. Not the companies. The companies would need to petition for the spades, without any pre-existing rights.

By applying this holistic view to today, with every single influence and credibility tool around, if you make several of your online profiles private, you will have low scores and be seen as non-influential. Even if you are influential. The poison lives on.

Many years ago the music industry decided to run a survey to see which guitars were most popular by region in terms of distribution and sales. To be included in the survey each manufacturer had to permissively share their unit sales. One particular manufacturer refused to do so, and that was Fender. The problem was, without Fender in the survey the rest of the data was immediately unrepresentative as Fender had a massive impact on the trend analysis.

I feel the online influence industry is destined to be a partial component in a fuller picture. Currently the buzz is loud enough to skim over the cracks, but take either of the scenarios above and the cracks are poison canyons.

The question then is: What is the maximum level of incompleteness that accuracy can suffer? After all, companies that are seeking to identify influencers surely aren't willing to discount chunks of real-life influence? Surely they aren't taking what happens on a handful of channels and assuming that's anything more than a micro-fraction of the picture?

No, I'd imagine that once the dust settles and the cool, funky technology has become yesterday's spiky haircut, the proper companies will address this game from an unsiloed strategic place, rather than an online-only viewpoint that tactically assumes what happens digitally is in some way more important or relevant than what happens in total.

Accessing the power of influencers and nurturing armies of fans is mission critical in today's business environment. However the technologist methodology belies the psychological requirements of modern assessment and engagement. When you're a hammer, everything looks like a nail – and when you make software, everything can be answered in a programme. Life, however, does not work like that.

There is simply no brand and no system, however cool, that can beat the physiological and sociological realities of how people relate, decide and act. Yes, tools can provide us with some information, but I implore you to see that incompleteness for what it is. Some isn't necessarily all. Online influence isn't necessarily all influence. No data gathering equals all actionable insight without addressing points that are seldom related to digital environments alone.

"The worst form of inequality is to try to make unequal things equal"
Aristotle

12. THE POISON OF PRESUMED CENTRALISATION

On November 16th 2010 an article appeared in Harvard Business Review (HBR), written by James Allworth, about Google's strategy. The gist of the piece can be gained from these two enclosing sentences; the first from the start, the second from the end:

1. "…But Google may regret the strategic choices that have led to this victory over Apple."
2. "The Android operating system is, as Google initially intended, untethered to any particular partner. This was a smart way of fighting the opening battles of the smartphone wars against Apple."

Basically the author is saying that mobile handsets with Google's mobile operating system (Android) are out-shipping Apple's iPhone due to Google's free distribution through what is called the Open Handset Alliance, yet this openness means there is no control over third parties choosing non-Google services instead, thus diminishing Google's competitive position.

In my opinion this critique of Google's supposed competitive strategy is entirely dependent on a context of traditional and centralised business practice. I believe this context is questionable. For it to be the case, Google would be displaying certain personalities of traditional centralisation, such as the need to control distribution or directly attack competitors, for example.

When things are centralised, ownership and enclosed resilience is vital; as what you have to hand defines your central unit of power. If Google traded in such a way, the HBR article would be contextually accurate and the opinion based on a valid conceptual construct.

However, Google is not a fully centralised business and their practice is fundamentally unlike many of the companies that commentators would seem eager to pitch it against. Allow me to clarify.

There are three types of organic business structures:

1. Centralised businesses (just as centralised organisms in nature) have a core hub and externally dependent spokes like a spider does. All behaviour, including competitive behaviour, is focussed on increasing the power of the core hub and decreasing the risk of the core hub being destroyed, which would end everything as all vital parts are within the core.

2. Decentralised businesses (just as decentralised organisms in nature) have all vital parts distributed throughout like a starfish does. There is no dependency of any part on any other. In fact, the further distributed it is (like when you cut off a starfish leg), the more the organism continues to grow. The starfish grows another leg, and the cut-off leg grows into a starfish. It's like Agent Smith in The Matrix. Remember?

3. Hybrid businesses are, unsurprisingly, a combination of centralised and decentralised architecture. In Google's case, as a hybrid business, there is centralised decision-making and decentralised execution. It is the decentralised execution that positions Google in a different way from their most obvious competitors (who tend to be extremely centralised – Apple for example).

Due to the common misinterpretation of their organic structure that leads to what I believe to be fundamentally inaccurate assessments of competition strategy and risk, I feel compelled to illustrate a different reality than portrayed in the original HBR article, and by doing so, address what I call The Poison Of Presumed Centralisation.

In 1943 Peter Drucker was commissioned by General Motors (GM) to investigate and interpret the secrets of their success. For 18 months Drucker probed and questioned all parts of the organisation and finally published his findings, as agreed he would, in a book called 'Concept of the Corporation'.

Due to the findings GM were very angry and Drucker was very surprised at this reaction. After all, in his book, Drucker had praised GM for their way of working, even likening them to the US Government's 'Federal Decentralisation'. Drucker said: "In Federal Decentralisation a company is organised in a number of autonomous businesses." Just as the US Government ceded power to the states, GM let go of central power to autonomous, decentralised divisions.

Drucker's advice was for GM as a hybrid organisation to become even more decentralised. He claimed their success was primarily due to the level of decentralisation. Drucker suggested such measures as hard-coding customer feedback into deep strategy.

But no. GM hated it. Their response was, in essence, "We are at the top of the game so why should we change?"

By the way, the Japanese car manufacturers took a far more proactive approach to Drucker's advice and the rest, as they say, is history.

Around this time, Drucker spoke of an organisational position that is often referred to as 'the sweet spot'. The place where organisations or offerings are centralised enough for control and commercial reality, yet decentralised enough for mass adoption and agility.

Google, with their decentralised execution, currently resides in a sweet spot of openness and pervasiveness.

Decentralised execution cares nothing for the supposed 'risk' of other players. In fact, the concentration is on creating tools for competitors to be empowered.

Did Google arm their competitors? Absolutely. On purpose.

Decentralised execution cares nothing for 'market share' of specific technology. Instead, the concentration is on becoming invisible, yet always there. The point of the story of GM and Drucker isn't about the reaction. It's about the empirical competitive advantage of decentralisation.

Despite unarguable evidence, the most common thought is that businesses are similarly structured with selfish centricity. The presumption by most commentators, including those in respected publications, is that companies are as centralised as spiders and compete accordingly. This is pure poison and shows an ignorance of business structure and market dynamics.

The poison is, however, extremely common. In the (absolutely vital) book, 'The Starfish and The Spider' by Ori Brafman and Rod Beckstrom, the second principle of decentralisation is: "It's easy to mistake starfish as spiders."

The frequency of commentators and competitors mistaking decentralisation for centralisation actually helps the decentralised compete. Put another way: The more that people misinterpret and treat decentralised companies as centralised, the bigger the threat. This is one of the main reasons that decentralised companies will rarely, if ever, correct a commentator or competitor who mistakenly uses centralised constructs in their reasoning. It is better for a starfish that others think it's a spider.

Despite this reality, The Poison Of Presumed Centralisation can be found everywhere. Another example can be found in an article called 'The Truth About Google's So-Called Simplicity'. In this, the commentator writes of confusion over Google's product range:

"A long time ago, 1968 to be precise, a wise person named Conway wrote: 'Organizations which design systems ... are constrained to produce designs which are copies of the communication structures of these organizations.' So true: I can see this in products from many a company. Except with Google, there appears to be no organizational structure of the product. Hmm."

The poison lives on healthily, demanding a level of naivety to exist.

In closing, and to be fair to the HBR article, one thing I would like to raise is what Google's strategy would be if they actually felt under attack. To quote again from Brafman and Beckstrom, the first principle of decentralisation is: "When attacked, a decentralised organisation becomes even more open and decentralised."

The message therefore is clear. Not only can we predict less predictability in competitive moves under attack, we can be assured that The Poison Of Presumed Centralisation will continue to empower the hybrid and decentralised. Faced with this reality, whom would you bet on to win?

13. THE POISON OF PLENTY TIME

Sometimes I get to speak with people about the future. This may be a future marketplace, a future product or future positioning that may be of benefit to an organisation or individual. Even when such futuristic talk is requested, many will cross-reference potential concepts with current key performance indicators or present-day demands from shareholders, bosses or other stakeholders.

When this happens, the futuristic talk runs the risk of being seen as even less realistic than it actually is. The most common outcome I observe is when a futuristic concept is accepted to be a likely outcome but is seen as a long way off. What this really means is that it isn't linked to today's metrics or their personal performance indicators, therefore it is irrelevant to people in business until:

1. They are measured on it and therefore motivated to act upon stimulus, or
2. Their company is commercially threatened by not having been previously involved (which normally means a competitor has already done it, leading to false comfort in knowing of a business case that exists – i.e. The Poison Of Proof), or
3. They have assumed a timeframe of maturation which is predominantly based on their level of historical reference, technical advancement or personal bias

This final option is the most concerning as it embeds a mind-set of having lots of time before needing to think or do anything different. This is what I call The Poison Of Plenty Time.

In 1965, Gordon Moore, the Co-Founder of Intel, wrote a paper predicting that the number of components in integrated circuits had doubled every year from their invention in 1958 until 1965 and predicted that the trend would continue moving forward toward Atomic level.

Five years later, a professor named Carver Mead coined the term 'Moore's Law' and since then the observations have turned into expectations across the technology industry, resulting in a self-fulfilling prophecy... although Moore did remind us that "it can't continue forever. The nature of exponentials is that you push them out and eventually disaster happens."

The technologically centred self-fulfilling prophecy has had a profound effect on many if not all industry verticals and now anyone over the age of 20 can probably remember products, services, tools, platforms and even companies that seemed like they would be around forever, only to be mutated beyond recognition or removed from the market completely.

One of the other poisons, The Poison Of Certainty, plays a strong hand in this. Experts are full of seemingly robust predictions, delivered with such certainty that many will continue to pay for them, even when the certainty is proved to be uncertain. The Poison Of Plenty Time pauses constructive change and innovation, it pauses curiosity and enables others to compete freely, whilst you sit on your hands.

The Poison Of Plenty Time is clever as it silences the rational part of the brain that could easily see that planning and implementation may take a number of years so the time period predicted actually implies action now rather than when the game has already been won (or at least started).

The Poison Of Plenty Time is so subtle that it drip feeds an endorphin into your system that makes you feel comfortable in the present, rather than needing flexibility and adaptability.

If you suspect you or your company suffers from The Poison Of Plenty Time, here are a few things that may help:

1. Experiment with a scenario that moves a 3 – 5 year prediction to a 9 – 12 month prediction. What would you do and how?

2. Assume, just for a moment, there are already individuals or companies putting things in place that could fundamentally cripple you. What would you do and how?

3. Learn about markets that have had seemingly sudden changes that nobody predicted and look at the companies that took advantage. What did they do and how?

Sedit qui timuit ne non succederet

(He who feared he would not succeed sat still)

14. THE POISON OF ONE NUMBER

Comfort often comes from the security of knowing how things are done. Discomfort often comes from not knowing the way things may be done in the future. The only thing I can predict is that change happens, today is the slowest pace of change we'll ever experience and those most adaptive to change have the greatest chance of survival.

What may have taken decades or centuries to manifest into a market shifting change, can now take years, months or days. Past generations seemingly had more time to adjust thought, word and deed, to observe, understand and exploit change.

Those in the fortunate position of enabling companies to move forward, or representing new and yet unproven verticals, have the task of providing some sort of justification and logic to new paradigms. Sadly, however, much of the justification suffers from a tremendously dangerous poison: The Poison Of One Number.

This is a poison that threatens entire value chains. A poison that chokes innovation, misdirects global markets and is responsible for multitudes of companies going down in flames. What does it look like?

Here are a few examples of the poison out in the wild. See if you recognise any:

"Ladies and Gentlemen, our global target for the entire organisation is 7%. I want you to drill this into your heads, write it on your bedroom walls and tattoo it on your wrist. It's all about 7%. Not one percent less... or else!"

How about this one?

"It's a new channel, everybody is asking for proof and there isn't any. However, I need to find some... I just need one number from the selling side, and one number from the buying side... any number... it doesn't even need to be that accurate. But we can't just keep guessing anymore. Just give me one damn number!"

No? How about this?

"Ultimately, the purpose of the campaign is to sell 500,000 units. It doesn't matter how it's done. The brand guys will give you some crap about 'protecting the reputation' but they aren't like us. They get paid either way – whereas we have to sell or we don't get our rightful commission. So chaps: sell the hell out of it at any cost... but don't tell the branding guys what I just told you..."

The Poison Of One Number is a pandemic. It stretches across every town, city, country and continent in every single industry vertical on earth. How does it happen?

The three factors that feed this horrible poison tend to be (in no particular order):

1. The New: There is nothing the poison likes better than a new situation, a new channel or a new environment. The poison feeds on the newness because it knows that others will be asking for answers or solutions. Then, as your mind works out what needs to be done, the poison presents itself like a gift at Christmas, parading across your desktop with no clothes on. "You just need me," it says. "I can make all these issues go away, just come up with a single number and you will be admired far and wide for having such clarity of vision." Lovely, you think. Problem solved. Yet actually you have just made a terrible mistake.

2. The Pressure: A by-product of The New is The Pressure that goes along with it. However, it doesn't have to be new to be a pressurised circumstance. The Pressure tends to

come from above, mostly from those who need one number to report to others who demand one number. You see? The poison has already infected them.

3.   The Ignorance: Due to the attraction of simplicity, the poison preys on those who fail to see the bigger picture or the potential downsides of chasing one number. The Ignorance is the most damaging diet to feed the poison because the outcomes are compound. This is where the harm is really done because the poison partners with The Ignorance and infects itself into anyone who hears the one number. The number frames the mind-set of others who then either a) see the one number as so attractive that logic goes out the window (and all that matters is the number), or b) see the one number as so unattractive that the proposition or opportunity is side-lined. Either way the poison wins as nothing progresses positively.

Nothing good can come from The Poison Of One Number because business doesn't work in such a way that one number can be all that matters. In fact, chasing one number belies the other factors that are critical in making decisions. For instance, such emphasis can be placed on a cost saving, often meaning that anyone who is only a cost is put under threat. Usually the marketing department. Or, such emphasis can be put on a sales figure, often meaning that sales practices are based less on maintaining reputation and more on getting the figures in.

Either way, The Poison Of One Number erodes our prioritisation of our most valuable assets – people. It erodes our perception of the need for innovation. It erodes our appetite for risk. It erodes, ironically, the chances of reaching the one number and still having a valuable business that offers value to its clients, customers or consumers.

Commoditising complex businesses into one number is the same as stating that raising a child is basically down to ensuring he or she has three meals a day. The number is 3 and that's that. That's all that matters, that's all we are chasing. If we hit the number 3, the child is worthwhile, but if we don't, the child is not. Ridiculous... and exceedingly common in how I see many companies being run.

In a new market, such as mobile advertising, many organisations build business models based on the following formula:

Total advertising spend = x

% advertising spend on mobile = y

% of market share achievable by us = z

Or

Volume of inventory we think we have = x

CPM value of inventory = y

Margin within inventory we should earn = z

Obviously I have simplified these somewhat, but nevertheless, they represent how the majority of business models start. The problem is that they revolve, at some point, around one number that generates the rest of the equation. In the first formula, the % spend on mobile tends to be the one number. In the second formula, the volume of inventory tends to have that pleasure. Then the poison gets to work.

The current % spend on mobile, as it is a nascent channel for advertising, is often low – sometimes 10% of digital which is 10% of the whole. Therefore, the poison promotes a fairly easy opinion that the market is too small to bother with. Or, in the second formula, the perceived volume of inventory is too high (as mobile operators view their millions of subscribers as millions of 'eyeballs' willing to tolerate adverts on their personal media devices). Either way, the rest of the calculations lead (quite often), to alarmingly unwise business decisions, investments and behaviours.

It's not that you shouldn't base your decisions on numbers. It's just that there are so many other factors involved which aren't as 'easy' to quote and seem too complex to understand — especially if you are an engineer of a technology firm, who has been told you now work for a "media company".

The main and seldom discussed factor is that paradigm shifts (as in the case of commercial communications in ultra-personal media) are rarely incremental. The fact that 10% of 10% is the current spend, may or may not bear any similarity to the state of the market in 6, 12, 18 or 24 months.

What can be done?

Bearing in mind that the poison is the sneakiest, nastiest, subliminal and attractive entity, trying to avoid it is a bit like the suggestion you never look up at the sky. It sounds do-able in principle but extremely unlikely.

Unfortunately, avoiding the poison is more psychological than that.

If I said that you would contract a horrible disease if you ever thought of a tree, regardless of looking at one, you would have no idea how to stop yourself. Actually, stopping yourself thinking of trees demands thinking of trees right?

Well, it's the same with this poison.

Every signpost in your business is asking you to focus on a number. A sales figure, a cost saving, a head count, a profit margin. So how on earth will you avoid The Poison Of One Number?

My advice is as follows:

1. Accept that you need to have numbers, but ensure there is more than one and they exist in different contexts – for instance, a sales figure complemented with a brand perception level of positive sentiment

2. Ask more questions of the numbers you are given, or that you arrive at

3. Avoid companies, circumstances, people and propaganda that are blatantly resting on one number, which, by the above definition, is almost certainly doomed for failure. If you cannot avoid them, then please be good enough to educate them. It's not their fault they have been infected with the poison – they probably work for someone who is highly contagious. Help them out of the hole with logical and structured reasoning that opens up a new way forward.

15. THE POISON OF OMNIPOTENCE

Sometime around 500AD, Pseudo-Dionysius the Areopagite asked whether it was possible for God to "deny himself".

The question was arguably the first emergence of what is called 'The Omnipotence Paradox' which states that:

If a being can perform any action, then it should be able to create a task it is unable to perform, and hence, it cannot perform all actions.

Yet, on the other hand, if it cannot create a task it is unable to perform, then there exists something it cannot do.

Whilst it may be enjoyable to venture into a debate on whether or not it is possible to ever be omnipotent, the fact is, it's tremendously attractive to imagine having unlimited, universal power. Not just as a person but as a business too.

I see numerous companies express monstrous capabilities to appear more competitive. Check out some of the halls at pretty much any exhibition and you will see stand after stand of slogans and tag lines including terms like 'end-to-end', '360°' and 'total'. I see products launched that, allegedly, are super-powered. I see services launched that, allegedly, will solve even the most challenging needs.

I wonder how much pressure comes from potential customers who, especially in new concepts, seek companies who 'do everything', citing economies of scale and efficiency as justification. I wonder how much pressure comes from competitors who claim omnipotence thereby forcing you to do the same to stay competitive. The whole thing feeds itself. Bigger and bigger claims, mostly based on sand.

Numerous agencies in the advertising world claim to be the 'world's greatest' this or that. The 'home of' something or other. The writers of such statements often believe the words to be true, even if nobody else does. One could argue that such expressed omnipotence is an internal communication tactic, making staff feel as if they are in the right place to work. Here's the deal:

I feel there is no long-term benefit of outputting claims of ultimate power or capability. In fact, claiming this is a very bad idea in many ways, and I call this The Poison Of Omnipotence. Of a cast of thousands, here are the three biggest disaster zones with this poison:

1. Over-promising. This is perpetually linked to under-delivery. Even if a deal gets won by some whizz-bang claims of extreme ability, the execution stage will be ever more painful. This is very pertinent in the current world of new advertising formats where minimum revenue guarantees are requested by potential customers who, frankly, should know better, and providers who, frankly, should do too.

2. Believability. In new areas where customers may not know what would be possible, you would think you could get away with seeming to be omnipotent. However, once levels of awareness and understanding increase, it's only a matter of time until the parameters are better known. Then you are in big trouble.

3. Trust and Integrity. This is totally impossible when the first two minefields come into play. Trust can only come from positive interactions, augmented by consistency and honesty, which builds integrity: the mother of all goals in reputation. In the long run, it would be better to have trust and integrity than to live in the hope you never get found out for not being the omnipotent force you seemed to be. You may do less business, but you won't be hated, derided and unable to function in the business world.

So, what is the antidote to this poison?

1. Leave it. I truly believe it's best to leave your competitors to kill themselves off, suffering from the three areas outlined above. Then you will still exist and have a clearer market.

2. Differentiate. Do this by not claiming to be omnipotent. Focus on what you are fantastic at. This isn't to say you should limit yourself, but only market competencies if you actually have them. If you think you need them to compete, then learn or buy them – but don't claim you have them if you don't.

3. Change perspective. Most companies follow competition. Markets are defined by this. This is why we so often are in a race to the bottom, trading in lowest common denominators, blindly competing for prizes that are evaporating. Just because the market seems to be going one way, that doesn't justify you following it.

One final thought: If you actually are omnipotent, or do have ultimate capability in your space, then the competitive advantage you have will express itself, through people. By telling everyone you have superpowers, you will simply look like all the others who say they do too. Leave them to make the claims, and you can get on with being fabulous. The truth will eventually come out. All you are is what you are.

16. THE POISON OF OLD WORLD PR

In the past, Toyota's safety warnings and vehicle recalls have provided succinct case studies in the realities of old world PR in a society of high speed information.

You may remember the one where, after two weeks of deafening silence, the Global CEO Akio Toyoda finally made a statement… only to be driven away in a black Audi. You literally couldn't script it. Yet another punch-line distributed across the world to hundreds of millions of people within seconds.

Meanwhile in the UK, Toyota comms chief Scott Brownlee was forced to admit the company was aware of problems 13 months prior, and sweated out a super awkward Channel 4 news interview, where even the most cynical would have felt sorry for the guy. That is, until he confirmed to PRWeek that Toyota would not be seeking external crisis advice in Europe. Another victim of The Poison Of Omnipotence perhaps?

But even if such crisis advice were in place, structural preparation is critical for every company. The reactionary approach to PR simply doesn't fit with the speed and efficiency of today's ultra-connected world. Some corporations tend to manage PR in-house and are known for waiting until all the facts are in before making a decision, let alone taking action.

Even before this ultra-connected society, the reactionary stance and cautious approach that companies like Toyota had taken increased the risk of others spreading a one-sided or ill-informed version of events. Now, an eventual reaction is more complex than a press release; it has to address the constantly moving and unseen targets of unauthorised information, often from a public armed with weapons of mass communication. The eroded trust can take years to re-build, if it actually does at all.

Today, the time taken for perception to change, en masse, is hours not days and definitely not weeks. It will be interesting to see how many more companies have to experience disasters like this before realising that their entire PR mentality needs to be re-booted. The speed and efficiency of public versioned stories out-paces and out-distributes all traditional means. It is not a minor issue that the general public are increasingly able to create, edit and publish. Now it is time all organisations realise this and fundamentally adjust their strategy, or live in a perpetual recovery period.

17. THE POISON OF INCOMPLETE LOGIC

In my opinion incomplete logic is one of the main reasons people fail in business. Smart people, nice people, experienced people with only one thing missing; the absence of complete logic in strategy, structure, process, culture, communications or methodology in general. I'm talking about the logical parts that are often unsaid. The parts that people assume that someone, somewhere in the organisation is taking care of, until they realise that everyone thought it was someone else's problem.

Incomplete logic can be vertical (i.e. a lack of depth in logical reasoning) and/or horizontal (i.e. a lack of breadth in logical reasoning) as illustrated below in the answers to a common question – "Your target is to get to 1 million product sales, how are you going to achieve this?":

Answer 1. "Through advertising"

Answer 2. "This particular social network"

This is The Poison Of Incomplete Logic. Recognise it? The main issue with incomplete logic isn't the chosen rhetoric. The answers don't need to be longer, provided they already contain a subject, transitive (or intransitive) verb and an action. The issue is that the answers illustrated above tend to be chosen by the responder as the complete answers. That's the problem.

For instance, following on from the first answer above, one could then ask: "How will advertising sell a million products?" and a typically incomplete response is:

A: "Because lots of people will see our advert and our product is so cool, people will want to buy it."

To which a question could be: "How many people will see the advert?"

A: "We can buy 10 million impressions, really cheap."

Let's push slightly harder to reveal the entire incompleteness of logic: "So that means 1 in 10 page impressions will need to generate a sale?"

A: "Yes… but that will happen because our product is really cool!"

The logic has run out of track. It is purely subjective, without a shred of credibility.

Now let's look at the second answer. Again we begin by testing the underlying logic: "How will this particular social network help you get 1 million sales?"

A: "People on this particular social network go crazy for this kind of product – once they see it they will buy it."

To which a question could be: "How are you going to find the people on this particular social network who will go crazy for it?"

A: "Create a page on this particular social network."

Going a bit deeper: "So once the page is created, how are you going to attract the attention of potential fans?"

A: "Word of mouth."

A bit more: "Who is going to spread the word?"

A: "Our head of social media."

Let's push slightly harder to reveal the entire incompleteness: "So one person is going to spread the word on Facebook and generate enough interest to sell a million products?"

A: "Yes… but that will happen because our product is really cool!"

The logic has run out of track. It is purely subjective, without a shred of credibility.

On an almost daily basis I get asked to make an introduction to someone in a theoretically powerful position. Actually, I don't get asked that question directly; I tend to get asked, "Can we meet for a coffee and a catch-up?" Which 9 in 10 times actually means, "Can we meet up so I can tell you about our business and you can provide me with contacts and/or sell our products and services for commission?" I tend to pass.

Over the years, I have noticed a worrying trend: the people who think they require contacts and sales, more often than not are riding on incomplete logic in one or more sectors of their business plan or organisation. However, one could argue, their situation may be as follows:

1. Many companies think they are sitting on a truly unique product
2. Many companies believe that sponsorship or advertising will be a major revenue stream
3. Many companies aren't connected to potential sponsors or advertisers
4. Many companies need help in sales and business development

But when asking those companies what their product does, where they add true citizen value, or how they could scale, the answers often lack the logic required to even consider introducing them to anyone who (to be honest) would instantly ask the same searching questions.

I see companies who have decided to get into Mobile Advertising for instance and after speaking with them for two minutes, you can tell the logic is all in bold 'heading' font. I see companies who have decided they need a social media strategy and have somehow confused the word strategy with tactic or channel, then wonder why it doesn't work out several, expensive, months or years later.

There is nothing underneath many of these players. It's all surface, no feeling. Huge gaps in logic ranging from essential sciences like 'how to create on-going dialogue with citizens' through to 'how to provide a value exchange' are covered over with massive charts showing algorithmic growth curves and glossy pictures which look incredible when projected onto a large screen at conferences, but under questioning fall apart.

But, to be fair, without knowing what you don't know, how can you tell what is needed? If you are an expert in your field already, surely you can be an expert in other fields, right? Surely the current vendor for solution X can equally be a fitting vendor for proposed solution Y? Especially if the vendor says they can do it (which almost all vendors do, regardless of capability – remember The Poison Of Omnipotence?).

This is probably the most common logic oversight; especially in a fragmented market where every day a new capability is added to a company's 'skill set', mostly because the rest of the competition is doing it too (ah yes, our old friend The Poison Of Proof).

It's extremely concerning when an entrepreneur, investor and/or employer is placing significant bets that are missing vital, invisible, logical ingredients. Now, as we know, those invested should push harder to get to real, tangible evidence that these bets can pay off – but the problem is, the 'newer' media is shrouded in hype and there is a lack of proper, solid business cases. Most skim over gaps in logic as it's too damn hard or complicated to address the very points that will determine whether something will fly or not.

It is all too easy to get sucked into the magnificence of a multi-million valuation that belies any real profit visibility, let alone revenue. In contrast, many in Silicon Valley claim a good business move currently is to get millions of 'eyeballs' and then work out how to monetise once you have critical mass – and even though you probably know that advertising is not necessarily the answer, it seems to be a great, simple model; 'build it and they will come'. I fundamentally disagree with this gap-ridden logic in the long term, so my advice for those entranced by this myth is to get in and get out quick, provided you can morally live with yourself.

Did you think the likes of Friends Reunited and Bebo could de-value so quickly? Even with a massive user base? The logic was incomplete. It ran out of track at the end of a shiny powerpoint and swanky office sofas. The founders sure as hell sold at the right time. It's interesting to see some founders buying back entities and applying the same logic as before for a second-wind of success. My advice again is to get in (again) and get out quick (again).

If, however, you wish to make a real difference, the risk in building a business with incomplete logic is far higher than building a business on solid, fundamental, reasoned, logical principles and processes. Incomplete logic is hard to identify and address. We need to question ourselves and question again, whilst being courageous and proactive. Without pontificating, we must scour our network of associates to sanity check every syllable we are pronouncing. Always ask how and why.

- Why are we really doing this?

- Why would people care?

- How can we add more value to society?

- How can we avoid arrogance and contentment?

We need to look in the cracks of our plans and propositions. We need to swallow our pride and ask the darkest, deepest and ugliest of questions. We need to get to the logical truth of it all, before we can try and persuade the rest of the world we have something worth celebrating. Never, ever stop this struggle. Be brave and do not under any circumstances allow incomplete logic to slide by under the surface. Start now.

18. THE POISON OF EXPECTATION

Have you ever been on public transport and seen someone eating a really pungent snack that made the entire area smell? Recently I sat opposite a guy who had a burger that embodied that description. He evidently thought it was appropriate to bring a stinking, greasy burger onto a packed commuter train. Would you ever dream of doing such a thing? Me neither.

Our expectation of what is reasonable frames our opinion of other people's actions. In our intrinsic desire ultimately for the world to work within the confines of our perspective, we spend a considerable amount of time frustrated at other people, other environments and other versions that do not fit our standards. This is The Poison Of Expectation.

We judge all the time. Someone isn't driving well enough. We could drive much better. Someone is walking too slowly. We always know when to walk slow or fast. Someone's house is way too messy. Ours is never that messy. We would never let it get into that state. Taking a smelly burger onto a packed train? Disgraceful, we would never do that. And now, assuming all citizens have the right to their own opinion, perhaps the people, who are accused in the above, also have an expectation of us that isn't being matched. We're too busy judging to know that, of course.

Maybe burger man thinks it's fine if others do as he does? Common courtesy is fine so long as you can define what common is and what courtesy is? These are subjective terms. Your personal hygiene standards may not necessarily be the same as the person sitting next to you on a 13-hour flight to the other side of the world. I have found.

But why is expectation a poison? After all, we're allowed to expect certain things, right? Well, the poison isn't about having personal aspiration; it is assuming that everyone would do what you do. The poison gets to work when we simply can't understand how someone has done something against our expectations, as we are basing our opinion solely on our own standards. This narrow lens creates an almost guaranteed level of confusion in our heads.

The Poison Of Expectation creates toxic fumes so we get more frustrated. It designs itself to move our focus from what matters. Even when we try to pull away and think objectively, the poison knows you will ultimately base your judgment on your own opinion, and by doing so, you keep feeding the poison.

The antidote to this is a tough one as it takes reasoning of other people's actions to disable the poison. Chuck D from Public Enemy once said, "If you can't change the people around you, change the people around you". Chuck's advice suggests two things:

1. To try and change the people around you (by educating, advising, helping or setting a different example)
2. To literally change the people you are around (by moving away from those you are unable to do the above with)

So, if burger man disgusts you, move carriages. If Captain Slow refuses to drive differently, change route. If our adjacent passenger isn't aware of the concept of washing, switch seats, use nose plugs or, (if you're brave), offer them your deodorant. Whatever you do, the one thing that leads to an endless negative vortex is to allow The Poison Of Expectation to eat you up inside. People are different. It's rare anyone will have the exact same standards as you.

19. THE POISON OF DATA BUBBLE IGNORANCE

On July 31st 2010, Doc Searls wrote a piece called 'The Data Bubble' – here's an excerpt:

"There is no demand for tracking by individual customers. All the demand comes from advertisers — or from companies selling to advertisers. For now. Here is the difference between an advertiser and an ordinary company just trying to sell stuff to customers: nothing. If a better way to sell stuff comes along — especially if customers like it better than this crap the Journal is reporting on — advertising is in trouble. Here is the difference between an active customer who wants to buy stuff and a consumer targeted by secretive tracking bullshit: everything. Two things are going to happen here. One is that we'll stop putting up with it. The other is that we'll find better ways for demand and supply to meet — ways that don't involve tracking or the guesswork called advertising. I've said it before: Improving a pain in the ass doesn't make it a kiss. The frontier here is on the demand side, not the supply side."

This issue is probably the most obvious in today's media industry and it represents my deepest concerns over the abuse of personal information. These concerns are central to my beliefs on how businesses should operate in an ethical way.

At the time of writing, 'Social Media' is one of the primary buzzwords and I believe the term is an invention from a business-opportunity standpoint. Social, because people socialise, and media, as there is inventory to be bought. The rich stream of private social data has resulted in many new billionaires, however I sense one of the most dangerous poisons hidden in the wings. This is The Poison Of Data Bubble Ignorance.

This poison could be rephrased (inelegantly) to: Ignoring the reality that hype-fuelled investment is creating unsustainable and illogical business models that are highly likely to fail.

But why would they be so likely to fail, and how could such wise investors miss the reality? One reason is that there are hundreds of thousands of people who are employed or funded to keep the bubble alive. Most of the people I know in the industry would and will disagree with much of this point, and from experience, it is not the most popular poison to discuss. From investors, to technology companies, to popular blogs and publications, through to advertising agencies and even Government departments; the bubble feeds itself with hype so thereby justifying its own existence.

The reality is that people don't want to be spied on. It's an abuse of civil liberty. The fact that people don't realise they are being spied on is not justification to do so. Betting on a business model that goes against how society really works will ultimately end in disaster. The gazillions of pieces of data that some social networks can aggregate to show increased targeting, is like a wet dream for those wishing to exploit this new social opportunity. The only people left out of this equation are citizens.

If you ask the people who are growing the poison by ignoring the bubble, their answers range from "consumers don't care about privacy anymore", to "consumers would prefer more targeted advertising – we are doing them a favour".

Actually, almost everyone ignores adverts in social networks – just as they do on any other digital page. You know what happens if you spy on people and serve more 'targeted' adverts? They begin to realise they are being spied on, and get freaked out. Yes, my friends, consumers are still human beings. So, what's the antidote to The Poison Of Data Bubble Ignorance?

The first piece of advice I can give is to read The Cluetrain Manifesto: www.cluetrain.com

The second is to seriously consider why you do what you do for a living. Do you want to make money regardless of whether you are actually acting in an inhumane way? Do you want to succeed opportunistically, making money while the sun shines, regardless of the potential downside afterward? Do you want to make a real and positive difference to people's lives (other than your investors, lawyers and stakeholders)?

Ask yourself.

20. THE POISON OF CERTAINTY

The more I look for it, the more I seem to find instances of people stating, with absolute certainty, what will or won't 'ever' happen. Look at TV companies stating that there will "always be TV" or music companies stating that there will "always be record labels". How about that there will "always be vinyl records" or that people will "always read paper books". These statements assume total knowledge of all future scenarios.

Actually, I suspect the correct interpretation is, "I cannot imagine a time when..." or "I have no reason to believe that..."

But people like certainties, explanations and tangibles. People like to speak and listen to assured advice. It's far easier to accept things if they are compartmentalised and well presented. The unpredictable is often seen as dangerous and threatening although I believe the main danger and threat is any level of assumptive certainty. That's the killer – that's the risk.

The next time you hear someone state that something will always exist, or never change; ask yourself how on earth they could know the future with such certainty? The past and the present have nothing to do with it. So what can you go on? Intuition? Luck? Guesswork?

Yes, it's awkward to do business without assured futures, so keeping sensory agility is critical. I'm certain it always will be.

21. THE POISON OF CAN'T

The fact is, we can't breathe underwater, unaided. We can't fly either. In fact, there are a number of things we simply cannot do. However, I suspect that most of our usage of the word 'can't' isn't actually related to things we literally cannot do. This presents the inaccurate use of the word can't as a poison, a misconception based on incorrect reasoning.

The main problem is that when we say, "Oh I can't do that", the thing we are speaking about gets compartmentalised in our brain, adjacent to being able to breathe underwater, unaided. Happy bedfellows, languishing in the vortex of the un-doable. Our mental filing system then requires extraordinary effort to switch folders from 'things I can't do' to 'things I possibly can do', which is why, after being told by someone that they can't do something, the work is so tremendously difficult in changing their opinion.

The Poison Of Can't is a nightmare to deal with. Of all the poisons, this is one that has the most extreme effect on progress, development and innovation. Stuff that makes people and organisations grow. The C word (as I sometimes call it – just to be on the safe side) is built into our language so deeply that we say it without realising and then the poison gremlin takes over. It sits waiting for you to say things like "I can't" or "We can't", then simply opens a mental drawer and plops the thing that you are talking about into it. Job done. It takes a nanosecond to do, and sometimes a lifetime to undo, if at all. If you're lucky, the folder system you have in your head has weak locks, meaning it's easier to re-file. But remember, weak locks are bad at keeping things in or out of anywhere, so you may be more susceptible to self-doubt.

When I was totally and utterly screwed over in business, losing pretty much everything in the process, I said, "I can't fix this. I can't make things better." But, over an arduous five-year period, I realised that I could. And I did. So how can one move from a can't to a can? Here's a quick and dirty checklist to combat The Poison Of Can't:

1. You need to define exactly what the thing is that you may or may not be able to do. Define it in exact terms. For me it was, on a human level, to be able to house, feed and support my family whilst not losing my mind in anxiety, stress and/or depression in the process. On a business level, it was to create an even better organisation than I had ever done before. On a moralistic level, it was to enable others to also reach their own potential.

2. Forget the tactics, forget the ways and means – first address a cold, hard question: "Is it humanly possible to do this thing?". If the answer is no, your challenge changes from one of struggle to one of acceptance and adaptation. If the answer is yes, your journey begins, but it may be a 2000 or 20,000 day journey.

3. Now you've established what the thing is and whether it is possible, it's now time to map out the separate steps you would need to take so you can start your journey. These steps should be achievable but you may find there are several sub-steps or dependencies. Then, you just have to get busy. If you have a barrier, refresh your answers to the points above. Remember, provided what you are trying to achieve is literally possible, it is down to you how successful you are.

For me, the above was my antidote for The Poison Of Can't. Whatever level of this poison you experience, in others or yourself, try and avoid the C word wherever possible. It produces zero net benefit for anyone. Life is too short to eliminate the possible.

22. THE POISON OF BINARY COLLABORATION

Extreme collaboration can be seen in the likes of Mozilla, Wikipedia and other open source platforms but the approach isn't just for the techie crowd. Companies like Muji, Lego, P&G and Starbucks have all got their heads (and organisations) around collaboration and are enjoying the upsides.

However, one of the main reasons other companies don't collaborate is due to the misinterpretation of what collaboration is and does. But even when companies get clarity, the risk is that collaboration is seen as a binary choice:

Option A: Don't collaborate so retain control

Option B: Collaborate so lose control

Obviously with these choices, many will choose option A.

Actually, collaboration doesn't need to be so stark and binary. If you have the inclination to establish a process and manage the facilitation, you can ensure that collaboration doesn't mean giving away all your company secrets or letting things get out of control.

Plus, not every part of your brand/company/solution needs to be part of collaborative efforts. Ergo, it's a poison to view collaboration in black and white, hence The Poison Of Binary Collaboration.

The four areas in which collaboration show the most obvious benefit are:

1.   Product Creation (from test-and-learn efficiencies)

2.   Customer Acquisition (from early-stage engagement)

3.   Loyalty & Advocacy (from organically shared ownership)

4.   Research & Insight (from combined learning and insight)

This is non-exhaustive. Every part of the value chain can benefit from collaborating with others. For those infected by The Poison Of Binary Collaboration and who wish to remain so, your main effort must be in ensuring the standalone company is omnipotent, force-fielded and super-powered. However, for those who wish to harness the energy and expertise of others and see collaboration as a multi-coloured, non-binary approach with unlimited permutations and extreme competitive advantage, the future is bright. Ignore this poison and move onward.

23. THE POISON OF ANTI-PIRACY LITIGATION

29th July 2011 saw fabulous news in the film industry. Finally, a way of addressing these pesky pirates had been found! In what has been termed 'a landmark case', an Internet Service Provider (BT), was forced to close down a site (Newzbin2). Lord Puttenham, the president of the Film Distributors Association at the time said, "It seems we have a way to deal with rogue sites". The inference is that this ruling opens the possibility of further actions against other Internet Service Providers.

In my opinion what is really going on here is the absolute infection of one of the worst poisons to hit the modern world: The Poison Of Anti-Piracy Litigation. This is the categorically mistaken belief of benefit, re-balance or reconciliation, from dealing with piracy via legal action as a primary approach. The infiltration of this poison will shape the future of the film industry, and many afterward. You may recall the music version, and believe me, some of us put forward the reality – but nobody was really listening.

Now a disclaimer: In case you think this chapter is pro-piracy, it isn't. Whilst I claim that suing pirates is a poison in terms of effectiveness, I do not condone illegality in any sense. As a published artist I'm amongst the people who are materially affected by piracy, so please take this into account as you digest the below.

Here's the deal: Attempting to shut pirates down via legal action is ultimately sub-optimal. However, the poison is massively widespread. It is commonplace yet one of the most illogical methodologies. But why is legal action against pirates so mistaken and unrealistic?

The practice of piracy is not based around a controlled head-office or hierarchy. There is no commercial instruction that drives it. The volume of piracy is unknown, the target is constantly moving, and the practice is a shared ideology that powers the decentralisation. This poison is a sister to The Poison Of Presumed Centralisation in that respect. The Internet Service Providers would never realistically be able to stop all piracy, and the command for them to do so shows an extreme lack of understanding of how decentralisation works.

Worse still, the removal of one particular 'rogue site' empowers other 'rogues' to be more 'rogue-like'. The only thing you can guarantee is that closing one, opens another. You have what is known as The Pirates Dilemma (the book of the same title by Matt Mason is a must read by the way). As piracy increasingly changes the way we find, use and sell information, how should we respond? Do we fight pirates, or do we learn from them? Should piracy be treated as a problem, or a whole new solution?

In my book "28 Thoughts On Digital Revolution" there's a chapter on counter-terrorism entitled "A Sect Cannot Be Destroyed By Cannonballs". In this I outline three ways in which such decentralisation can be attacked, assuming you decide to attack rather than concentrate on the potential. These are paraphrased from another critical book called 'The Starfish and The Spider' that I cited in The Poison Of Presumed Centralisation.

1. Change the pirates' ideology by showing them another, better way
2. Centralise pirates by giving constructs for greed to be built
3. Decentralise yourself

Sadly, many institutions, associations and policy makers have been infected so deeply with the poison that the above falls on deaf ears. What actually happens is they do the same thing over and over again (i.e. sending lawyers after pirates), expecting a different result. Einstein called this the definition of insanity.

From the recent news, the expected outcome for the film industry will be the reduction of lost revenue. However, the actual outcome will be the continuing reduction of revenue, aided by the funding of expensive legal teams. What they should be doing is working out how to monetise in a new world, or how to use the pirates as an advantage. They should be accepting that the old world of control and traditional business has changed, and also that the societal trend is towards content being free.

I strongly suspect they won't and the piracy will continue, along with the demise of the traditional entertainment industry as we know it. Meantime, ask yourself: When this type of disruption comes to your industry, what will you do? I only ask because the chances are that disruption is already underway. The fact you can't see it is part of the challenge.

24. THE POISON OF THE ADEQUATE

The story starts in a busy restaurant in Surrey, with a queue snaking out of the door against steamy windows. The time was 7.45pm.

The maître d', flushed, rushed and crushed by a hungry mob demanding answers (and feeding), hastily assured us the waiting time was 45 minutes and directed us to the serving hatch, usually reserved for waiting staff as opposed to waiting diners.

The assured 45 minutes came and went but alas, few tables became available. Meanwhile, dozens of people flowed in and joined the masses by our designated hatch for waiting, blatantly obstructing the service, but with no other location to dwell.

A lucky few were eventually seated. It turned out they had earlier bookings that, upon arrival, were found to be largely irrelevant to seating availability. After 90 minutes, people who had got a table started walking out, muttering aloud about the poor service.

I spoke to the manager at the end of the evening and he claimed that "9 in 10 times" such over-subscription worked fine – sales rocketed and everyone was kept "relatively happy". He claimed that this time was the rare occasion when things didn't quite work out and were "pushed a bit too far".

In reality, nobody was happy. Not even relatively. The waiting staff, kitchen and bar staff were stretched beyond their limit and one could see they weren't exactly impressed. The customers were mostly furious and I counted five tables who walked out without paying. Who knows the negative word of mouth that will come of it, and frankly I doubt many will return, not until the management changes perhaps.

Let's rewind to the horrifying attacks of the 11th September. When the plane reportedly crashed at the Pentagon, those requiring emergency treatment were rushed to the hospital only to find a similar situation to the restaurant in our first story. The problem was that the hospital normally ran at 95% capacity and disasters over a certain scale were simply not catered for. One could argue that the scarcity of disaster validates the lack of preparation – although that argument probably didn't do much to placate the injured and the families of those involved.

What we see, time and again, is the creation of mechanisms and systems that are only adequate if predictable things happen. The problem is, the damage caused in terms of reputation when the "rare occasion" happens, is often at a greater scale than the positive stuff in normal circumstances. Due to this, playing an adequate majority game ("9 in 10") is not only dangerous, it's a lethal poison: The Poison Of The Adequate.

So what can be done? Is it practical to resource for the unknown? Well that depends on your interpretation of what resourcing requires. For our restaurant manager, having 45 extra tables hidden away and an automatic mezzanine floor that extends over the diners' heads may not be realistic. For our hospital directors near the Pentagon, the same contraption may not be within reason either – but think about what they both could have done.

Disaster planning, within the wider realm of scenario planning, is in two parts, both of which are proactive:

1. Systems put in place that reduce the chances of situations occurring
2. Systems put in place that come into play if or when certain situations occur

My ludicrous example of extendable mezzanine surfaces would reside in the second of these two. However, an example of reducing chances would be if the manager had stopped new arrivals, apologising profusely but politely turning people away. For sure, the situation would not have occurred and right now, dozens of people (including me) wouldn't be relaying negative stories about the night.

The hospital near the Pentagon could have a pre-arranged agreement with local schools perhaps, ensuring emergency use of sports halls and tables. Maybe even a few other hospitals could pool together an emergency supply of essentials that could be drawn upon if needed. Volunteer staff who are known and contactable before a crisis happens.

Ultimately, the reason people don't have plans in place for the unknown is because of a three-way perception of risk, damage and time. We tend to assume there is a low risk of the unknown happening, with a low level of potential damage if it did – but either way, unlikely to happen anytime soon. Actually, there is no evidence to support this.

If anything, in hindsight following a disaster, we see there was probably a relatively high chance it was going to happen at some stage, often sooner rather than later, and with a relatively large amount of damage. We are perpetually surprised. Such is The Poison Of The Adequate.

In today's world we have new types of disasters. Take, for example, a 'social media crisis' where a brand is dilapidated by society conversations and insufficient or incompetent involvement by the brand's representatives. Like the restaurants and hospitals beforehand, many companies have a low perception of risk, damage and time even whilst smugly observing other companies destroyed by freak events. "It will never happen to us – and if it did, we would handle it," they say.

Very few organisations choose to be proactive, understand potential damage and create protocols to reduce the chances of disaster. The primary characteristic is naïve reactivity amongst those who are playing a roulette game of chance, quietly praying the ball never lands on their number.

CONCLUSION

In general, these poisons prey upon a lack of preparation and action. Many say they know what's going on, yet few actually do and this is one of the most popular reasons why the most powerful organisations in the world are being infected by business poison. I genuinely hope that this volume can counteract the impacts if possible.

If I were to be a motivational writer, I'd say that now is your chance to observe whether you or your organisation has ingested one or more forms of business poison and make the necessary counter moves as fast as possible.

As I'm a realist, I'll guess that you already know if you or your company contain any variety of these poisons. Whilst I cannot judge, I genuinely hope that you feel it is appropriate to take personal accountability in attempting to counteract your own mix of modern business poison.

For those who do, a healthier business future awaits.

Good luck.

If you are interested in continuing your thought expansion, you can join Jonathan's 'Thought Expansion Network' (also known as TEN), which offers cutting edge insight and expert opinion via video content, masterclasses and live events.

Join TEN now at: jonathanmacdonald.com/ten

Printed in Great Britain
by Amazon.co.uk, Ltd.,
Marston Gate.